Zen Doodling ORIGAMI

Carolyn Scrace

BOOK HOUSE

Published in Great Britain in MMXVI by
Book House, an imprint of
The Salariya Book Company Ltd
25 Marlborough Place, Brighton BN1 1UB
www.salariya.com
www.book-house.co.uk

ISBN: 978-1-910706-41-1

SALARIYA

1 3 5 7 9 8 6 4 2

A CIP catalogue record for this book is available
from the British Library.

Printed and bound in China.

Every effort has been made to trace copyright holders. The
Salariya Book Company apologises for any omissions and
would be pleased, in such cases, to add an acknowledgement
in future editions.

CONTENTS

INTRODUCTION
Zen Doodling

CAPTIVATING

Anyone can Zen Doodle! It's enormous fun and will get your creative juices flowing but beware... it can be addictive! Zen Doodling stimulates your imagination and enhances your daily life. The captivating results will build your artistic confidence and develop your design skills.

MEDITATION

The repetitive nature of drawing patterns not only produces a stunning piece of art, it is also very therapeutic. It encourages relaxation and acts as a focus for meditation.

REWARDING

Learn the process of deconstructing a complex pattern into simple shapes that can easily be replicated. Follow the simple easy-to-follow instructions then doodle incredible patterns.

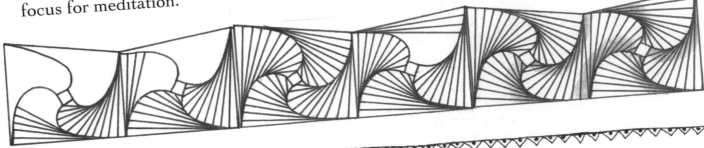

Origami

ANCIENT ART

The ancient art of origami has been practised in Japan for over 1,000 years. The name origami comes from two Japanese words, *ori* meaning 'folding' and *kami* meaning 'paper'. Originally, the Japanese Imperial Court used origami as an amusing way to pass the time. Over the years, it became popular with Japanese people in general, eventually developing into the international folk art that it is today.

Discover how you can transform a simple square of paper into an incredible origami animal or beautiful box, then embellish your creation with stunning Zen Doodle designs.

This book contains 20 sheets of origami paper in delicate colours together with easy step-by-step instructions for making 12 stunning models.

Note: the origami paper is coloured on one side only.

ORIGAMI BASICS

Symbols and Their Meanings

Valley fold

Fold sides together to form a 'V' shape.

Mountain fold

Fold sides together to form an inverted 'V' shape.

Fold back

Fold paper towards the back of the origami.

Turn over

Turn the origami shape completely over.

Rotate

Rotate origami shape by 90°, 180° or as indicated.

Tuck inside

Tuck inside part of the origami shape.

Important Origami Base Folds

KITE BASE

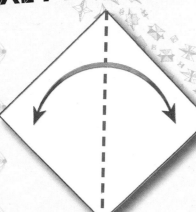

1 Make a vertical valley fold. Unfold.

2 Valley fold the sides into the centre.

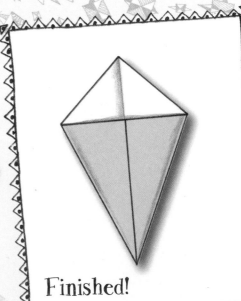

Finished!

SQUARE BASE

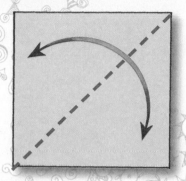

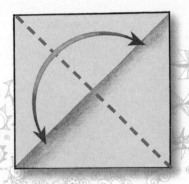

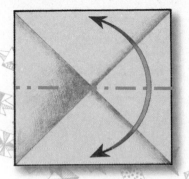

1 Valley fold the paper in half diagonally. Unfold.

2 Valley fold the paper in half diagonally the other way. Unfold.

3 Mountain fold the paper in half horizontally. Unfold.

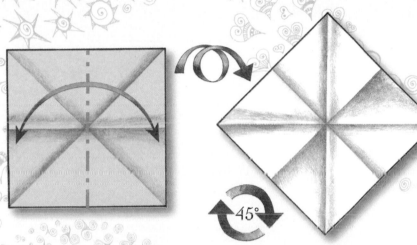

4 Mountain fold the paper in half vertically. Unfold.

5 Turn the paper over, then swivel it round by 45°.

6 Start to bring the top and two side corners down to meet the bottom corner.

Finished!

7 As the paper folds it should look like the drawing above.

8 Press the square base flat.

LUCKY RABBIT

BEGINNINGS

The rabbit is a powerful symbol of spring, new life and fresh beginnings. Many people believe the rabbit to be very lucky. In Japanese myths and folklore rabbits are closely associated with the moon.

1 With the pink side up, fold the kite base (page 6).

2 Rotate 180°.

3 Make a horizontal valley fold.

4 Valley fold the top downwards (as shown).

5 Now rotate 180°.

6 Valley fold the bottom point to align with the top edge.

7 Crease all folds firmly.

8 Use scissors to cut as indicated.

9 Valley fold in half vertically.

10 Rotate clockwise to lie horizontally.

11 Valley fold the upper layer as indicated.

12 Turn over.

13 Valley fold the top layer as indicated.

14 The rabbit should look like this!

Viewed from above:

15 Open up the base so the rabbit will stand.

15 Carefully pull open the rabbit's ears.

Finished!

PAISLEY PATTERN

CLASSIC DESIGN

Paisley pattern is a classic design using a teardrop or tadpole shape. It originated in Persia over 2,000 years ago. Paisley continues to be a very popular pattern for fabrics, accessories and with trend-setting fashion designers.

EXPERIMENT

Lay the origami rabbit flat on some scrap paper and trace round its outline. Experiment with different designs for doodle patterns. The teardrop shape of the Paisley pattern is ideal for the rabbit's front and back legs.

Rough sketch

Incorporate a moon into the design.

CONTRAST

Use predominantly black, white and silver Zen Doodles. For dramatic contrast, add bright red patterning to the legs on one side of the rabbit only.

Rough sketch

Step-by-step deconstruction of Paisley pattern one:

Paisley is much easier to doodle than it looks. Start by drawing an inverted teardrop shape, and then break the pattern down in simple stages.

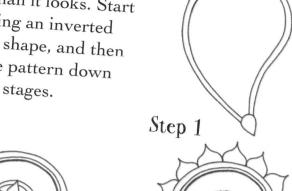

Step 1

Step 2

Step 3

Step 4

Step 5

Step-by-step deconstruction of Paisley pattern two:

Step 1

Step 2

Step 3

Step 4

Step 5

Step 6

11

Rabbit Doodles

Open out the origami rabbit and lay it flat.

Lightly pencil in the main shapes of your design. Go over these lines with a black 0.1mm fineliner pen. When the ink is dry erase the pencil lines.

Simplify the rabbit's face. Draw its features in black and embellish with silver gel pen doodles.

STARTING POINT

Treat your sketches as a starting point only - let your ideas change and adapt as you doodle! It's time to relax and enjoy Zen Doodling!

Use a 0.5mm black fineliner pen to fill in large areas. Red, fine-nibbed gel or fineliner pens are ideal for adding coloured details.

Take care when re-folding the finished origami rabbit!

13

FABULOUS FLOWER

FLOWER HEAD

Traditionally, origami flowers have been given as gifts of friendship and love. This simple origami also makes stunning interior decoration. Vary the shape of the petals to create a wide range of flower designs.

1 Start with the white side of the paper facing up. Fold the square base on page 7.

2 Rotate 180°. Valley fold the top layer inwards as shown.

3 It should look like this. Then turn over.

4 Valley fold the top layer inwards as shown.

5 Pencil in the shape of a petal.

6 Use scissors to cut out the petal shape.

7 Valley fold the bottom point up (as shown).

8 Crease then unfold.

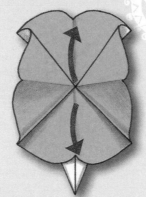

9 Fold down, then spread open along the dotted line.

10 Ease the top and bottom petals outwards.

11 Then flatten flower.

ORIGAMI LEAF AND STEM

1 With the white side of the paper facing up, fold the kite base on page 6.

2 Valley fold both sides into the centre.

3 Valley fold the sides into the centre.

4 Make a vertical valley fold.

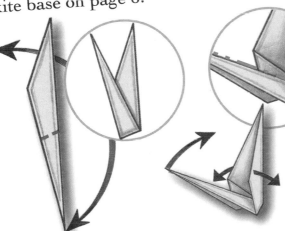

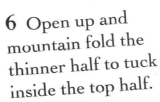

5 Valley fold the bottom up at an angle (as shown). Crease and unfold.

6 Open up and mountain fold the thinner half to tuck inside the top half.

Finished!

Artist's tip: attach the flower to the stem after the two origami models have been Zen Doodled.

MEANINGFUL

PANSY FLOWER

Throughout history and in cultures across the world, flowers have been attributed with symbolic meanings. Pansies are particularly associated with loving thoughts and remembrance. The flower's smudged markings and simple five-petal shape make it ideal inspiration for a Zen Doodle flower design.

COLOUR ROUGHS

Make colour roughs of your designs before working on the finished origami flower. Trace or sketch the paper flower and leaf onto scrap paper. Experiment with different Zen Doodle patterns and colour schemes.

DECONSTRUCTION

I like to deconstruct complex patterns into easy-to-draw steps.

Start by lightly drawing a pencil grid:

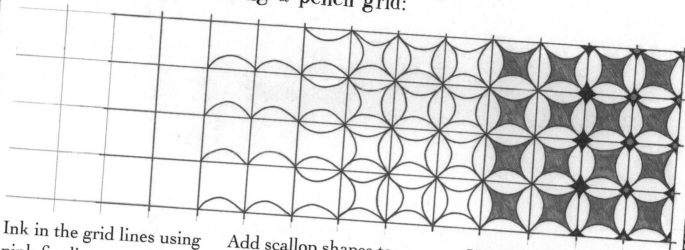

Ink in the grid lines using pink fineliner pen. Draw scallop shapes above and then below each horizontal grid line.

Add scallop shapes to either side of each vertical grid line. Colour in the background in the centre of each square (as shown).

Use black fineliner pen to draw a diamond shape where the lines cross. Add a gold gel pen dot in the centre.

Start by lightly drawing a pencil grid:

Use pink fineliner pen to draw alternate rows of thin, vertical scallop shapes. Alternating the scallop direction creates wavy vertical lines.

Draw rows of thin, horizontal scallop shapes. Alternating the scallop direction creates horizontal wavy lines.

Draw 3 diagonal, wedge-shaped lines through each centre (as shown). Add black fineliner dots at the end of each line.

IN THE PINK

BLOCKING IN

Take your origami flower and sketch in the main shapes of the flower design. Use a felt-tip or fineliner pen to block in the background colours.

Now relax and Zen Doodle!

Use pink coloured fineliner pens and pencil crayons to doodle the petals.

Draw around the heart shapes and borders using white gel pen to add tonal contrast.

Inner leaf

Outer leaf

Stem

Lightly pencil in your design onto the origami leaf and stem. Use black fineliner pens with white and gold gel pens to Zen Doodle the patterns.

18

PANSY FLOWER

Place the flower flat, facing down. Open up the base of the flower stalk and spread a tiny blob of paper glue inside. Position the tip of the leaf stem on the adhesive and refold the back of the flower. Hold firmly until the glue is dry.

Artist's tip: try gluing a length of thin metal wire (or an opened out paper clip) inside the leaf stem to give it added strength.

ORIGAMI BIRD

This beautiful, traditional origami bird design is very easy to make.

Artist's tip: first decide whether you want to fold a mainly blue or white bird, then turn the origami paper over accordingly.

1 Paper coloured side up, fold the kite base (page 6). Mountain fold the top point back.

2 Valley fold the top two corners down.

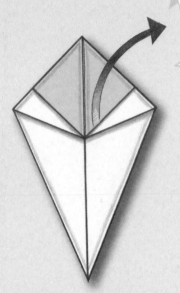

3 Unfold the right corner.

4 Ease the inside top corner out and reverse the fold.

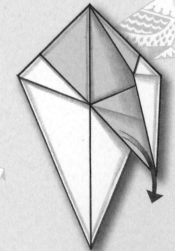

5 Continue to pull the corner down. Now flatten.

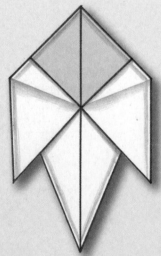

6 Repeat steps 3, 4 and 5 on the left side. Your model should now look like this.

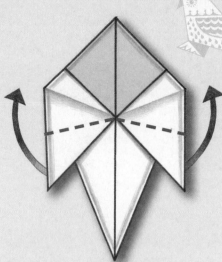

7 Valley fold the two side points up (as shown).

8 Valley fold the bottom point up to the centre.

9 Now valley fold the point down (as shown).

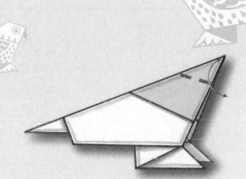

10 Valley fold in half vertically.

11 Turn round 70°.

12 Valley fold the top down. Crease and unfold.

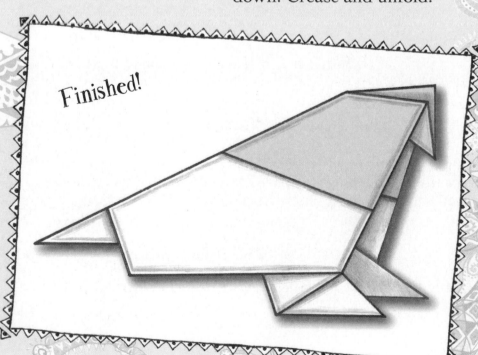

13 Ease the fold open slightly. Reverse the centre, fold and tuck inside.

Finished!

21

CURLS AND SWIRLS

CREATIVE IDEAS...

Take a square sheet of scrap paper and fold an orgami bird. Get creative! Work loosely, and have fun experimenting with different doodle patterns and designs.

Rule of thumb: for all the projects that follow, use layout paper, or any thin scrap paper you have to hand, for this stage of the design process.

3D origami colour sketch

To make these stand out tonally, I have used mainly black and gold for the bird's wings. This contrasts well with the paler doodles on its head and body.

3D origami colour sketch

Artist's tip: check that your tonal values work by squinting through half shut eyes at your bird design! Does it work?

22

INSPIRED BY FEATHERS

These bold patterns are inspired by the shape of bird feathers.

Start by drawing a pencil grid:

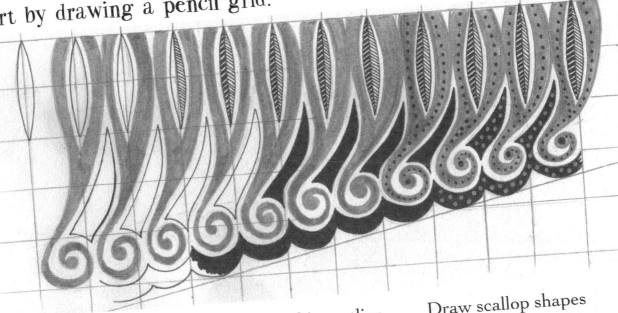

Use black 0.1mm fineliner pen to draw in a series of elongated leaf shapes.

Leaving a white outline, doodle in a long, curling design in golden brown. Use a fineliner pen.

Draw scallop shapes along the base. Fill in with black fineliner pen. Add stripes and spots.

Start by drawing a pencil grid.

Use a black 0.1mm fineliner pen to draw a row of scallop shapes. Draw a second, staggered row beneath. Repeat the first two.

Add small, black scallop shapes under each row. Add two more bands of scallop-shaped lines.

Add a pattern of straight lines that radiate outwards. Use gold gel pen to doodle in spots.

FUN DOODLING...

Open up your finished origami bird (Step 10, page 21), and turn it right side up. Lay the model flat. Lightly pencil in the main elements of your design. Add pencil grid lines where necessary. Now relax. Fill your mind with images of beautiful birds flying through the air, and get doodling! Have fun.

Note: I used white origami paper to fold this model.

COLOUR SCHEME

I have chosen to use predominantly pale blue and golden brown for the bird, with the addition of bold blacks and whites to add tonal contrast. To make the bird's eyes more noticeable, surround the pupils with bright yellow and orange.

TOOLS AND MATERIALS

Other than origami paper, there are no special tools needed for doodling origami. However, as the origami models in this book are small, I find black and coloured fineliner pens with fine nibs are ideal for intricate doodling. Felt-tip pens or marker pens can be useful for blocking in larger areas of colour. I also use white and metallic gel pens to add pattern detail onto darker shades.

FORTUNE TELLER
TRADITIONAL ORIGAMI TOY

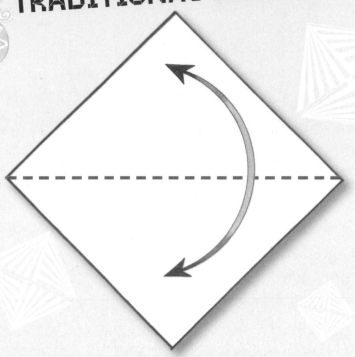

1 With the white side of the paper facing up, valley fold in half horizontally. Unfold.

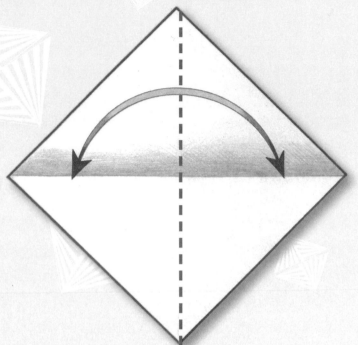

2 Valley fold in half vertically. Unfold.

3 Valley fold horizontally bringing the top point into the centre.

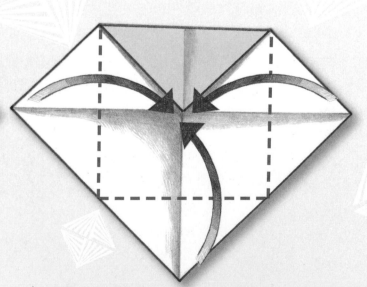

4 Valley fold the three remaining points into the centre.

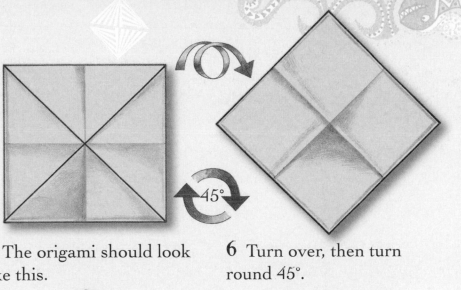

5 The origami should look like this.

6 Turn over, then turn round 45°.

7 Repeat step 3.

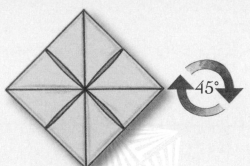

8 Repeat step 4.

9 Valley fold in half vertically and unfold.

10 Valley fold in half horizontally and unfold.

11 Turn over.

12 Lift up the centre flaps.

13 Insert both thumbs and index fingers into the pockets.

Finished!

14 Turn over. Use your thumbs and index fingers to open and close the fortune teller.

OPTICAL ILLUSIONS

WHAT IS REAL?

Optical illusions can use colour, pattern, or light and shade to create images that trick the eye into seeing something in a completely different way - an illusion! The Fortune Teller's 3D geometric shape is ideal for Zen Doodling with patterns based on optical illusions.

3D MODEL SKETCH

For this particular origami model it is useful to make a 3D sketch. Use scrap paper to fold a fortune teller, then experiment to try out different Zen Doodle designs.

ROUGH SKETCHES

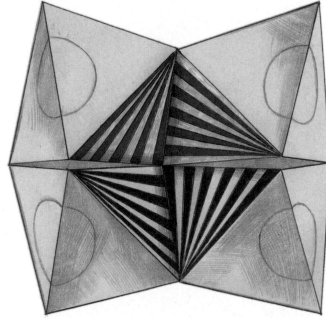

I've used converging stripes with added shading (page 34) to make the pattern appear to weave in and out.

Here, I've created an illusion of depth, by progressively making the stripes thinner and closer.

EYE-POPPING DESIGN

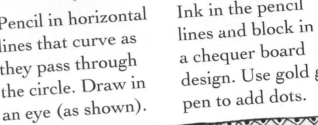

Pencil in a horizontal and vertical line to locate the centre. Use compasses to draw a circle (as shown).

Pencil in vertical lines that curve as they pass through the circle area (as shown).

Pencil in horizontal lines that curve as they pass through the circle. Draw in an eye (as shown).

Ink in the pencil lines and block in a chequer board design. Use gold gel pen to add dots.

EXPERIMENTATION!

Try drawing different types of eyes: reptilian, feline or human - experiment!

Try out different colour schemes - a yellow-green eye with a yellow and black pattern, or perhaps reds and yellows.

Shading

To make it appear more 3D, add shading around the outside of the eye-ball.

Turn to page 34 for a step-by-step guide to shading techniques.

Use a white gel pen to add highlights to the eyes.

Geometric Doodles
VIBRANT COLOURS

Open out your origami fortune teller and lay it flat with the coloured side uppermost.

Lightly pencil in the design. Use 0.1mm black fineliner pen to go over the lines.

Add shading using pencil or black ballpoint pen.

Block in main areas of colour with fineliner pens. Use contrasting colours such as red and green or black and yellow to add vibrancy.

Use a fluorescent yellow marker pen to block in the eyes. Colour in the pupils with black. Build up the colour of the eyes using fine dots in either pale green or orange fineliner pen.

ADDED IMPACT

Alternating the use of red and green in the side panels adds impact to the overall design.

LIMITED PALETTE

I have deliberately excluded blues and purples to restrict my colour palette. I find working with fewer colours helps me concentrate more on tonal quality when Zen Doodling.

31

ORIGAMI CICADA

SUMMER

Cicadas hibernate during the winter, then emerge to sing throughout the summer. In Japanese culture they symbolise reincarnation and intransigence, and are associated with the summer.

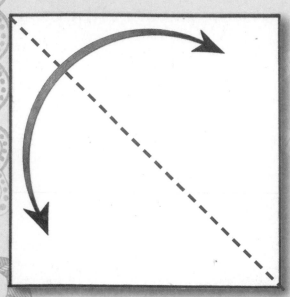

1 With the white side of the paper facing up, valley fold in half diagonally, crease then unfold.

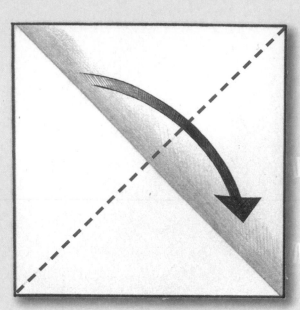

2 Valley fold in half diagonally.

3 Now rotate by 45°.

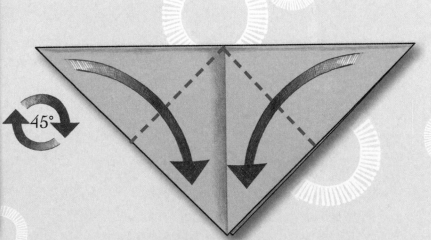

4 Valley fold the two corners down to the bottom point.

5 Now rotate by 180°.

6 Valley fold the two top corners down. Angle folds (as shown).

7 Valley fold one layer of the top section downwards (as shown).

3/4

5/8

8 Valley fold the next layer down (as shown).

9 Mountain fold the sides to meet at the back. Turn over.

10 The origami should look like this. Turn over.

11 Valley fold the two top corners.

Finished!

LIGHT AND SHADE

SHADING TECHNIQUES

Shading is a technique that artists use to add tone to an image or pattern in order to make it appear three dimensional.

Hatching

Pencil

Fineliner pen

Hatching builds up tone using a series of thin parallel lines. The closer together the lines are, the darker the tone becomes.

Mixed media hatching

Cross-hatching

Pencil

Fineliner pen

Cross–hatching uses two layers of angled hatching that cross to create a mesh-like pattern. Add more hatching to build tone.

3D Effect

To create a 3D effect on a 2D pattern or shape, choose the direction of the light source then add shading. Build up layers of tone leaving the lightest parts unshaded.

Light source

ORNATE DESIGN

Using scrap paper, I folded another origami cicada, to play around with different Zen Doodle patterns. I wanted to create designs that I could shade in to give the cicada a rich and ornate appearance.

34

3D PATTERNS

Helpful sequence...

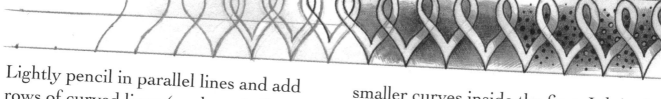

Lightly pencil in parallel lines. Ink in curved lines along the top and bottom

sections. Add pencil shading. Run a line of silver gel pen along each curve.

Lightly pencil in parallel lines and add rows of curved lines (as shown). Repeat curves in the opposite direction. Add

smaller curves inside the first. Ink in the pattern so the lines appear to weave over and under, then add pencil shading.

TEMPLATE

Sketch out a curling 'C' shape for a template. Trace it onto thin paper. Draw the template at different angles to create a design of overlapping shapes.

Ink in the outlines. Block in the background colour using fineliner pen. Add pencil shading then Zen Doodle with patterns.

SCALLOPS

Draw in a pencil grid. Ink in horizontal and vertical lines (as shown). Add a row of scallop shapes and fill in. Doodle triangles and semi-circles, then add dots.

SUBTLE EFFECTS

TOP AND BOTTOM

Open out the side folds of the cicada and lay it flat. Lightly pencil in the structure of the Zen Doodle patterns. Use a black 0.1mm fineliner pen to outline the main elements of the patterns. Stop doodling occasionally to fold in both sides and turn the cicada over to check how the patterns work on the underside.

Topside

Topside

Artist's tip: avoid smudging your artwork by resting your drawing hand on a piece of scrap paper.

Underside

ADDING DEPTH

Use whatever materials you like best to Zen Doodle. To create a subtle effect, I chose to work in fineliner and gel pens adding depth of colour and shading with pencil, pencil crayon and ballpoint pen.

36

DECORATION

To create this stunning, decorative feature, attach the origami cicada securely to a sturdy flower stem, well away from any moisture.

Underside

Topside

Use white gel pen to add highlights to the cicada's eyes and wings.

CELESTIAL BOX

A TRADITIONAL ORIGAMI STAR BOX

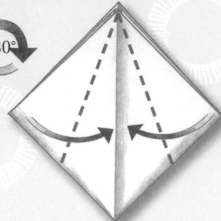

1 With the white side of the paper facing up, fold the square base (page 7).

2 Turn 180°. Valley fold the front layer into the centre.

3 Turn over.

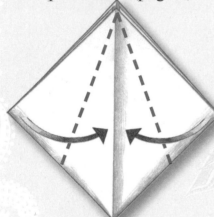

4 Valley fold again.

5 Valley fold both flaps.

6 Crease well and unfold.

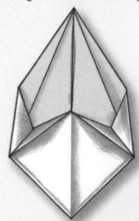

7 Lift both flaps up.

8 Tease open each flap. Then flatten.

9 Turn over.

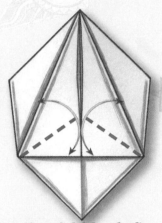

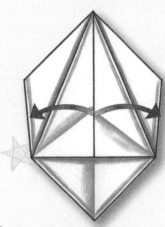

10 Valley fold both flaps. Crease well and unfold.

11 Lift both flaps up.

12 Tease open each flap. Then flatten.

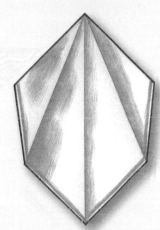

13 Valley fold the front layer from right to left.

14 Now turn over.

15 Valley fold the front layer from right to left.

16 Valley fold the top layers into the centre.

17 Turn over.

18 Valley fold into the centre again.

CELESTIAL BOX CONTINUED...

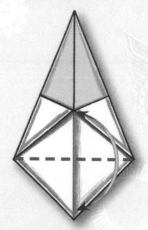

19 Valley fold the bottom up. Unfold.

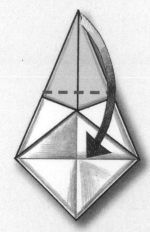

20 Valley fold the top layer down.

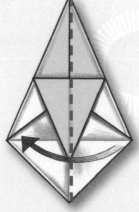

21 Valley fold the side (top layer) - right to left.

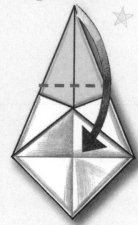

22 Valley fold the next top layer down. Turn over.

23 Valley fold the next top layer down. Fold the side from right to left.

24 Valley fold the last top layer down.

25 Gently ease the box shape open. Carefully flatten out the base.

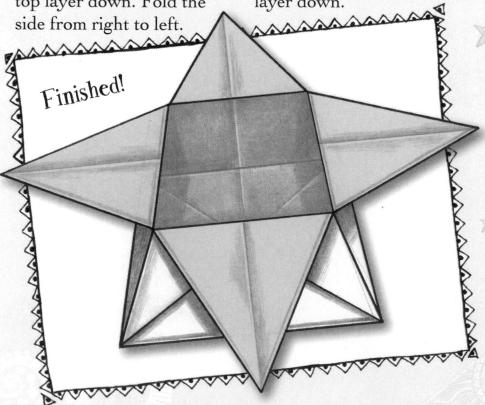

Finished!

SUN AND MOON

CENTRAL MOTIF

Start by making colour sketches. To create the central motif for the base of the box, combine the images of a sun and moon. Use colours that represent light and warmth to colour in the sun's side of your design. Use luminous, cool colours for the moon's side.

COLOUR SKETCHES

Experiment with different designs and colour combinations. The stylised yellow and gold sunrays become more striking with the addition of a dark blue background.

3D
origami colour sketch

41

Colour Temperature
Sunlight and Moonlight

Use hot colours for the sun: yellows, oranges and reds. Use cold colours for the moon: blues, blue-greens and purples. Now relax, and fill your mind with thoughts of glorious, warming sunlight and magical, mysterious, cool moonlight. Then start Zen Doodling!

Artist's tip: before unfolding the origami box, use a soft pencil to lightly mark in the areas to decorate. Gently open up the box and lay it flat, coloured side up.

1 Lightly pencil in your design. Go over the pencil lines with a black 0.1mm fineliner pen.

2 Block in the main areas of colour. I have used fine felt-tip pens, pencil crayons and fineliner pens.

4 Use gold gel pen to add curling doodle patterns to the sun's face and for the border.

3 Add pencil hatching to the face to make it look rounded. Start doodling the patterns.

REVERSE SIDE

Once the coloured side is finished, turn the paper over and Zen Doodle the sections that will form the sides of the box. I have used a simple pattern of gold stars outlined in black fineliner pen, then coloured in with gold gel pen. A background that is lightly shaded with coloured pencil works well when doodled with gel pen swirls.

When the artwork is dry, refold the celestial box.

43

Beautiful Butterfly

Origami butterflies have many different meanings in Japan. A pair of paper butterflies, for example, symbolises a happy marriage and plays an important role in Japanese weddings.

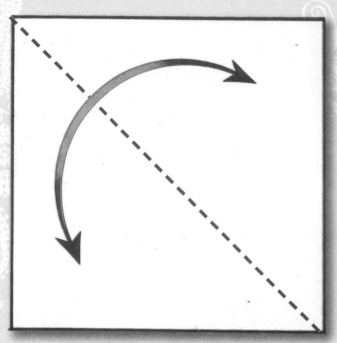

1 White side facing up, valley fold in half diagonally. Crease and unfold.

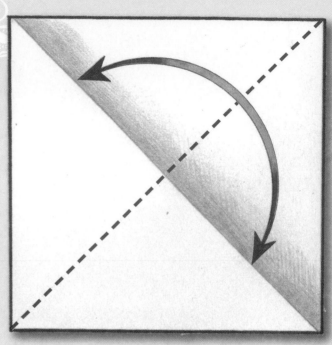

2 Valley fold in half diagonally. Crease and unfold.

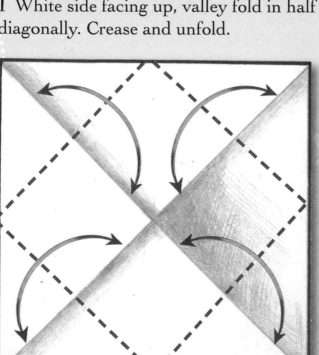

3 Valley fold the four corners into the centre, crease and unfold.

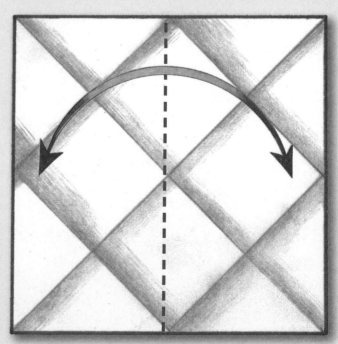

4 Valley fold in half vertically. Crease and unfold.

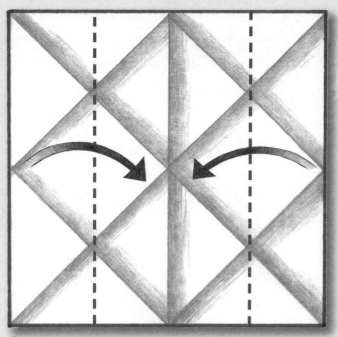

5 Valley fold the two sides vertically into the centre.

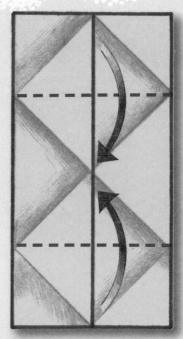

6 Valley fold the top and bottom edges horizontally into the centre.

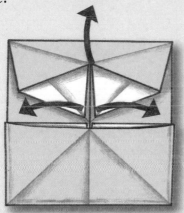

7 Start to lift up the centre (upper section) and ease out the corners.

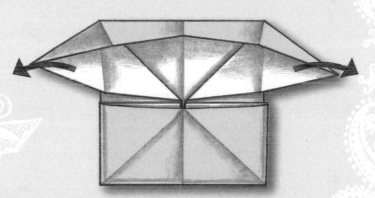

8 Pull out the corners and flatten.

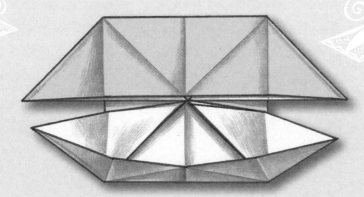

9 Repeat steps 7 and 8 to the lower section.

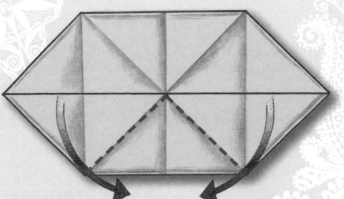

10 Valley fold the lower section down (see next page).

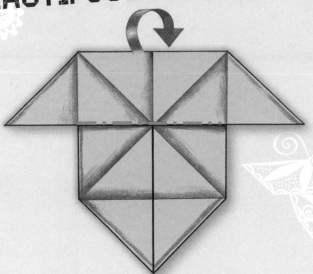

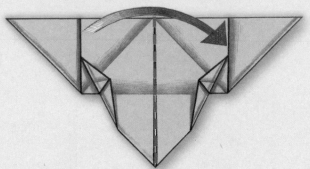

11 Mountain fold the top section backwards.

12 Valley fold the corners of the top layer (as shown).

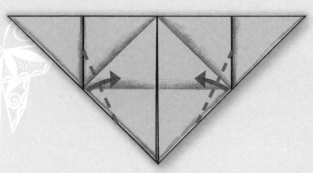

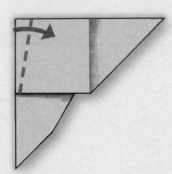

13 Valley fold in half vertically.

14 Valley fold the top corner (as shown) and crease firmly.

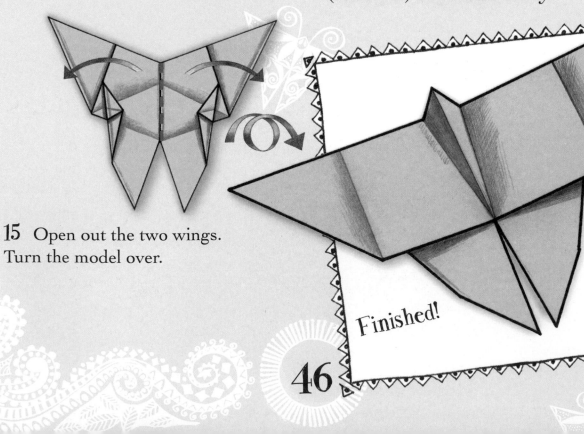

15 Open out the two wings. Turn the model over.

Finished!

BUTTERFLY WINGS

3D COLOUR SKETCH

Fold an origami butterfly out of scrap paper. Now have fun experimenting with designs for the wing patterns. I've used looping ribbon shapes to create a structure for the patterning on the top wing sections. Many butterflies have 'eye-spots' on their wings, so incorporating them into the design will add a dynamic element that reinforces the appearance of a butterfly.

COLOUR SCHEMES

At this stage, try out different colour schemes. This golden yellow, orange and red colour scheme works best on white or pale yellow origami paper.

DEPTH OF COLOUR

Build up depth of colour by layering a darker colour on top of a lighter one. For example, try adding cross–hatching (p 34), using mid-blue fineliner on top of sky blue pencil crayoning. Doodle on top using darker blue, turquoise or purple fineliner pens.

47

COLOURFUL EFFECTS...

DRAWING OUT

1 Lay the finished origami model flat, top side up. Then lightly pencil in the basic design on one half of the butterfly. Using tracing paper (or baking parchment), copy the design onto the other half.

Topside

2 Ink in the pencil lines with black fineliner pen.

3 Turn the model over and repeat the first two steps. Block in areas of black using fineliner and marker pens. To create a subtle effect, use pencil crayons in pale colours to shade the main wing sections, and add fineliner hatching to show depth.

Underside

Topside

4 Its time to relax, have fun and begin Zen Doodling. Although the main elements of the design are symmetrical, I have used different patterns to decorate each section.

5 I used bold black and white Zen Doodled patterns for the lower, underside wings to contrast with the delicate, pale doodles on the upper section of the wings.

Underside

48

6 Colour in the 'eyes', then doodle the butterfly's body.

FINISHING TOUCHES

To make the pale blue origami paper appear white, doodle over with white gel pen. Use silver and white gel pens to add the finishing touches to the doodle patterns.

FRAMED...

The completed butterfly looks stunning when framed. I made two blue origami butterflies, then Zen Doodled the topside of one and the underside of the other. The frame was one I had found in a second hand shop and luckily was the perfect fit for both models!

GOLDEN FISH

WISDOM AND LUCK

In Japan, the goldfish is believed to bring prosperity, power, wisdom and luck. Its image plays a vital role in much of Japanese art and culture.

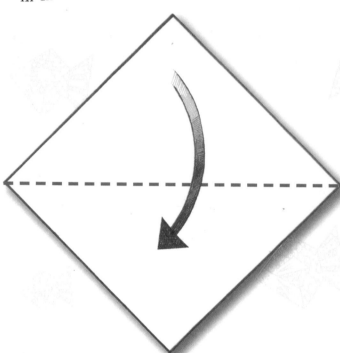

1 With the white of the paper facing up, valley fold in half horizontally.

2 Valley fold vertically. Crease and unfold.

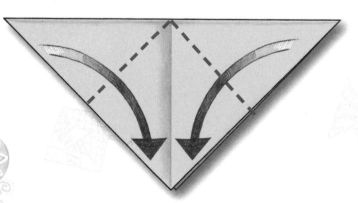

3 Valley fold the side corners down to the bottom.

4 Valley fold the top layer in half horizontally.

50

5 Valley fold the top sections down at an angle.

6 Valley fold the top layer horizontally (as shown).

7 Valley fold this section again.

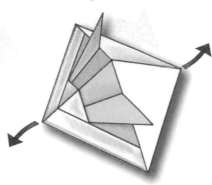
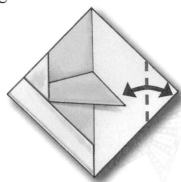

8 Mountain fold the bottom flap back.

9 Pull the front and back sections apart. Flatten.

10 Valley fold the corner, crease firmly and unfold.

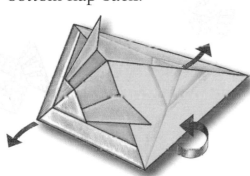
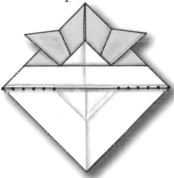
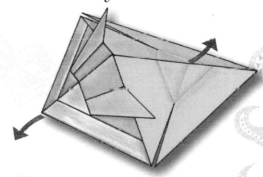

11 Open out the base, unfold the back flap (step 8), and flatten.

12 Use scissors to cut where indicated.

13 Partly open out the base.

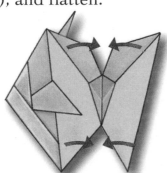

14 Push the crease lines inwards to ease the tail into place.

Finished!

SCALES AND WAVES
ZEN DOODLE EXPERIMENTATION

Use an origami fish made from scrap paper to rough out some basic Zen Doodle designs. Try alternating colour schemes - blue on yellow, then yellow on blue.

FISH SCALE PATTERNS

Start by pencilling in the lattice-shaped pattern of fish scales. Then try out different designs, colour combinations and materials to see which work best - experiment!

Block in the scale shapes with pale blue fineliner pen, then doodle using darker blue and black fineliner pens.

Pencil in the fan-shaped pattern of a fish's tail. Use its structure as a basis for Zen Doodling patterns.

Try out different variations on a theme: add lines instead of spots, or change the colour or direction of a line.

52

TONAL CONTRAST

Place thick black stripes next to areas of pale coloured doodles for tonal contrast and to create a bold design.

WAVE PATTERNS

Deconstructions:

Start with a lightly pencilled grid:

Draw a series of staggered, horizontal rows of curly lines. Add smaller curly lines to link each row with the one below.

Block in the curl shapes with a yellow fineliner and the background with an orange fineliner. Add doodled lines and dots using red and gold gel pens.

Start by lightly pencilling in three parallel, horizontal lines:

Ink in a series of equally spaced black dots along the centre line. Use the guidelines to draw curls to link alternate pairs of dots.

Draw a second series of curls that link with the first. Use yellow and black fineliner pens to block in areas of colour. Add doodle patterns using gold, silver and red gel pens.

FABULOUS FISH
RELAX AND DOODLE...

Unfold your finished origami fish, as shown in step 12 (page 51). Lay it flat. Pencil in the main shapes of your design.

Turn the model over and repeat. Use fineliner pens to outline the different shapes. Start blocking in areas of colour.

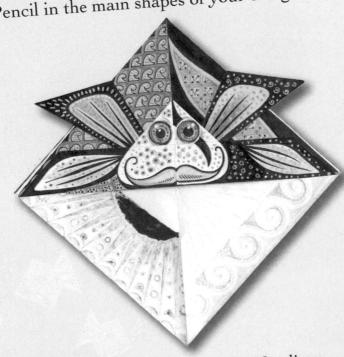

Add detail to the doodles using fineliner pens and gel pens.

Apply the finishing details with white and gold gel pens.

MOBILE AQUARIUM

Note: all these images show the same fish from different angles.

Instructions

Take two strips of card and cut slits as shown (above). Tuck a ribbon inside the top of each fish and glue in place.

Attach the ribbons to the base of the card strips. Add a ribbon to hang the mobile.

MAGICAL BOX

Start by making the lid of the box:

Note: you will need two sheets of origami paper to fold the magical gift box.

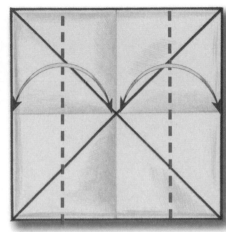

1 With the white of the paper facing up fold steps 1- 5 on pages 26-27.

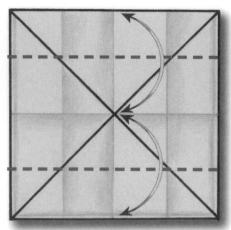

2 Valley fold the two sides into the centre, crease firmly and unfold.

3 Valley fold the top and bottom into the centre. Crease and unfold.

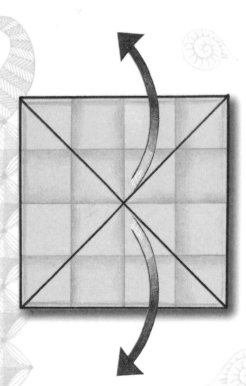

4 Open out the top and bottom triangles.

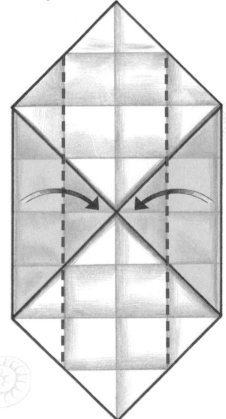

5 Valley fold both sides into the centre.

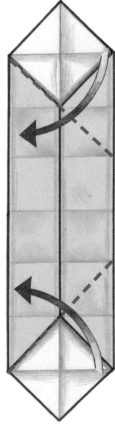

6 Make diagonal valley folds. Crease.

56

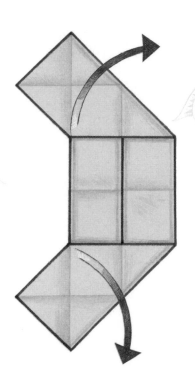

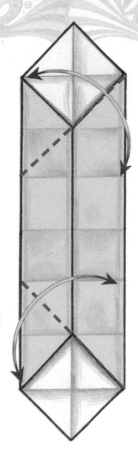

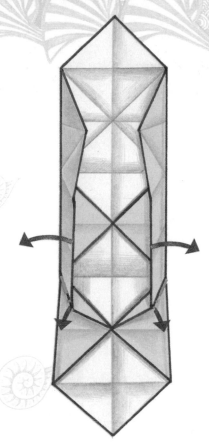

7 Your model should look like this. Unfold.

8 Make diagonal valley folds, crease then unfold.

9 Moutain fold along the two creases. As you fold the sides will open out.

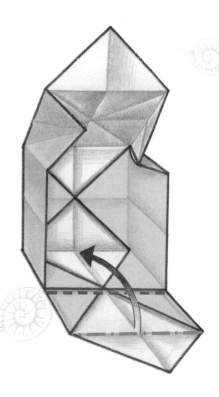

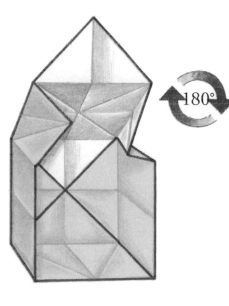

180°

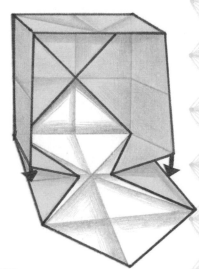

10 Crease flat. Valley and mountain fold the bottom flap inside.

11 Rotate 180°.

12 Bring the corners down to meet the bottom flap, then crease flat.

MAGICAL BOX CONTINUED...

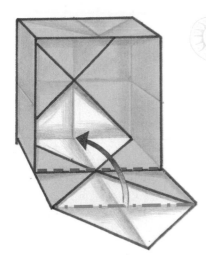

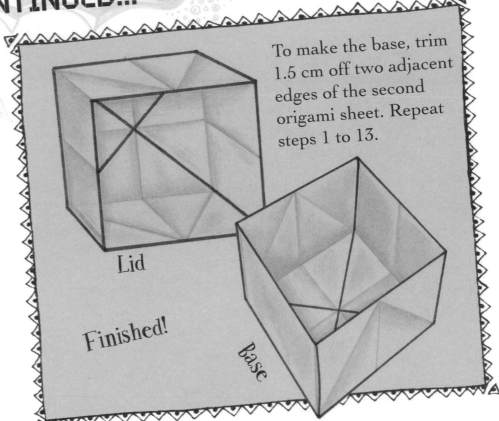

To make the base, trim 1.5 cm off two adjacent edges of the second origami sheet. Repeat steps 1 to 13.

Lid

Finished!

Base

13 Valley and mountain valley fold the bottom flap inside.

WOVEN PATTERNS...
SUPRISE ELEMENT

3D rough

Make another magical box out of scrap paper. As an experiment, I doodled patterns that make the box appear woven, like a basket. I decided to give the design a suprise element by sketching a Zen Doodled shell on the lid.

NO SUCH THING...

Woven patterns are great fun to do, but I find I need to deconstruct and practise them before starting on finished artwork. There is no such thing as a mistake when Zen Doodling. Embrace your errors – they add richness and interest to a design.

58

ZEN DOODLE PLAIT...

Pencil in three parallel guidelines. Add a row of short, angled lines with curved bases (as shown). Now pencil in the top row of angled lines with curved tops to form a plait (as shown). Use a fineliner pen to ink in the lines. Erase the guidelines. Add pencil and ballpoint pen hatching.

SQUARE WEAVE...

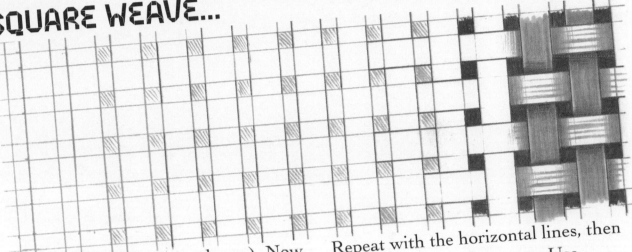

Draw a pencil grid (as shown). Now lightly shade in the small squares. Use black fineliner pen to draw pairs of vertical lines that appear to weave over and under the horizontals.

Repeat with the horizontal lines, then colour in the small squares. Use fineliner or felt-tip pen to colour in the vertical rectangles. For a 3D effect, add pencil and ballpoint pen hatching.

BASKET WEAVE...

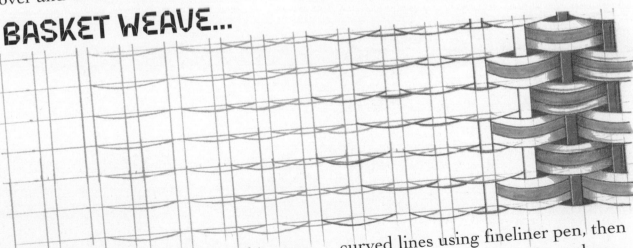

Lightly pencil in a grid. Pencil in rows of scallop shapes that weave over and under alternate sets of vertical lines (as shown). Pencil in more rows of scallops that cross over the first set. Ink in the curved lines using fineliner pen, then the vertical lines. Add stripes, then colour in with fineliner felt-tip pens. Use pencil and ballpoint pen hatching for a 3D effect.

PICNIC HAMPER

THE LID...

Use a pencil to lightly mark out the top and sides of your finished origami lid. Unfold it and lay it flat. Take your time, and use a ruler and pencil to sketch in the design. As the overall design is like an old fashioned picnic hamper, I carried this theme through to the inside by using a checkered pattern that looks like a picnic blanket. Go over the pencil outlines with 0.1mm black fineliner pen.

BLOCKING IN

Erase any pencil lines and start blocking in areas of colour. I used red and grey felt-tip pens for the checkered pattern and angled strips. To make the woven pattern look 3D, I left the centres of the yellow rectangles uncoloured as the highlights, then added shading at the sides using a combination of yellow fineliner and yellow pencil crayon.

THE BASE...

Zen Doodle the base following the instructions opposite. Repeat some of the patterns previously used on the lid to unify both parts of the box.

FINISHING TOUCH...

For the finishing touch to the lid, lightly shade around the shell. Use pencil and ballpoint pen to add a shadow.

Carefully refold the box and the lid and fit them together.

ORIGAMI TURTLE
SYMBOLISING LONGEVITY...

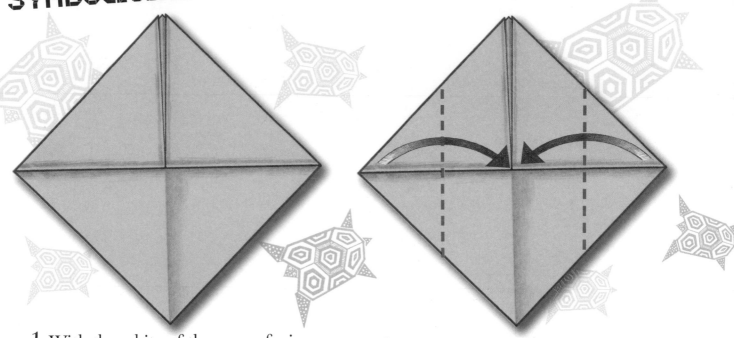

1 With the white of the paper facing up, fold up to step 4 of the Golden Fish on page 50.

2 Valley fold the two sides into the centre.

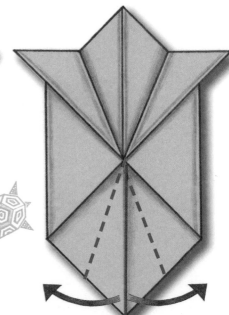

3 Valley fold the top two points out (as shown).

4 Use scissors to cut the top layer only (as shown).

5 Valley fold the bottom two points out.

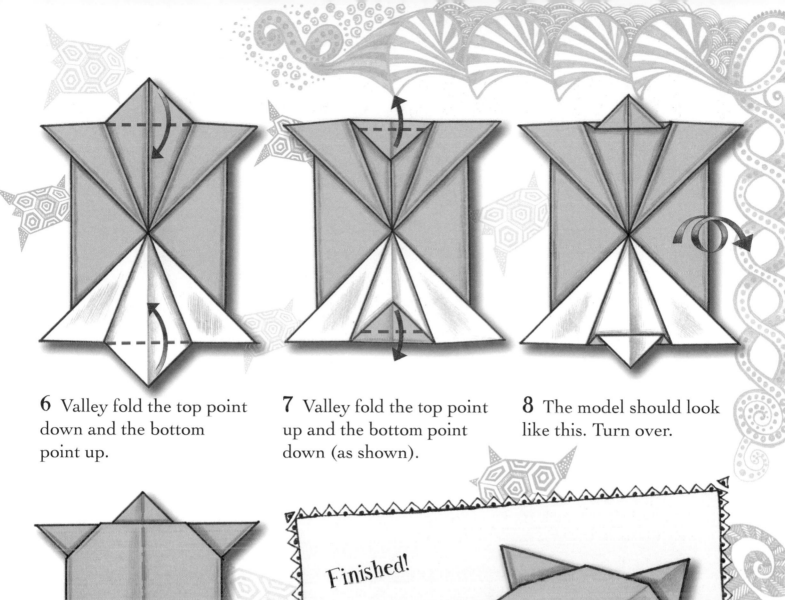

6 Valley fold the top point down and the bottom point up.

7 Valley fold the top point up and the bottom point down (as shown).

8 The model should look like this. Turn over.

9 Make a soft, vertical mountain fold down the centre so that the turtle stands up.

Finished!

GEOMETRIC PATTERNS
BLACK AND WHITE

I used the beautiful patterns of turtle shells as inspiration for my experimental Zen Doodle designs. I tried bold, geometric patterns to reflect the patterns on the turtle shells. Using stark black and white doodles, make the origami turtle shell stand out against the colour doodles restricted to the turtle's head and legs.

ROUGH IDEAS

Make rough sketches of design ideas. Use origami turtles made from scrap paper to try out different Zen Doodles. Block in areas of black with marker pen and try doodling on top with white or silver gel pens.

3D sketch

3D sketch

Rough sketch for shell design...

THE ILLUSION OF 3D...

This is one of my favourite patterns. It looks three dimensional and, once broken down into simple steps, is great fun to doodle.

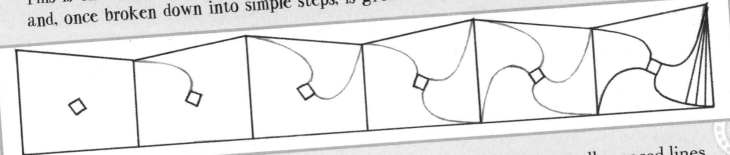

Ink in a four-sided rombus. Add a tiny, tilted square in the centre. Pencil in curved lines from each side of the small square to each corner (as shown).

Ink in. Start inking in equally spaced lines that fan out from the top right corner to meet the curved line below (as above).

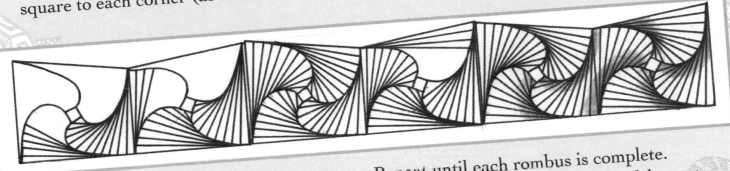

Turn the Zen Doodle 90° clockwise. Ink in another set of lines fanning out from the top right corner to the curved line.

Repeat until each rombus is complete. Add pencil shading to the areas of densest line work to reinforce the 3D quality.

Pentagonal version:

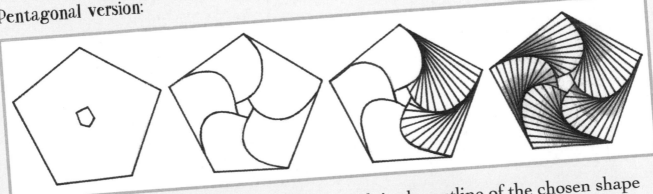

This Zen Doodle pattern can be adapted to suit almost any shape that has straight sides such as a triangle, pentagon or hexagon.

Ink in the outline of the chosen shape then draw a miniature, tilted version in its centre. Then repeat the same steps as described above.

TONAL CONTRAST
BLACK AND WHITE

To make your completed origami turtle easier to work on, partially open it up, then lay it flat. Feel free to adapt and combine elements from the previous designs as you pencil them in. Use 0.1mm black fineliner to go over the outlines, then relax and Zen Doodle!

The bold black border gives a strong frame to the design and adds to its tonal quality. As a contrast, I used soft pencil crayons to colour the background of the turtle's head and legs.

Draw in the turtle's eyes and Zen Doodle its face and legs using fineliner pens. Use black ballpoint pen hatching to shade in the darker areas of pen work on the shell. Use silver gel pen to add a simple pattern of dots to the black frame. Finish the head and legs with doodled dots in gold gel pen.

TURTLE FAMILY

Light source

Try making smaller versions of the origami turtle to create a turtle family. The 'young' turtle was folded on 15 x 15 cm origami paper. I chose simple, geometric patterns that would be easy to Zen Doodle on a smaller shell. To enhance the 3D quality of the shell design, first choose your light source then use black ballpoint pen hatching to darken areas furthest from the light.

Artist's tip: allow time for gel pen doodles to dry out. I am forever smudging my work!

SUPER STARS

Note: you will need a ruler, pencil and scissors to make the model.

Start by making an equilateral triangle:

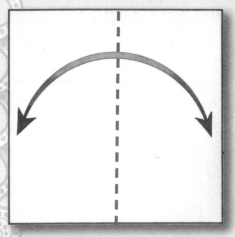

1 With the white of the paper facing up, valley fold in half vertically and unfold.

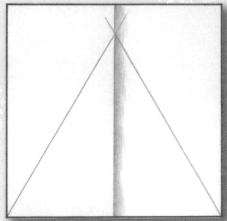

2 Draw lines (the length of one side) from the lower corners to the centre fold line.

3 Use scissors to cut out the triangle. Valley fold in half then unfold.

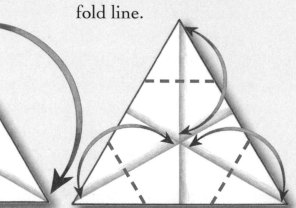

4 Valley fold in half then unfold.

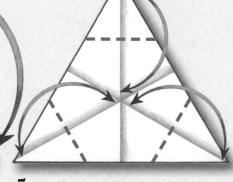

5 Valley fold the corners to the centre, then unfold.

6 Valley fold the top corner down, to base line.

7 Valley fold the point up (existing fold line).

8 Valley fold the bottom left corner up to the right.

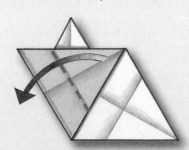

9 Valley fold the point down (existing fold line).

10 Valley fold the bottom right corner up to the left.

11 Valley fold the point down (exising fold line).

12 Unfold the right side and tuck the point behind.

13 Tuck the right hand fold line under the top section.

14 Bring the other corner on top of the left side.

15 The model should look like this. Turn over.

Finished!

SNOWFLAKES

INSPIRED BY SNOWFLAKES...

Snowflakes have six arms that radiate from their centre, making them the ideal inspiration for Zen Doodle designs for decorating an origami six-pointed star.

Rough sketch

Rough sketch

Using scrap paper, make sketches of the star. Divide each star in half, then try out different snowflake designs.

Traced design

Artist's tip: pencil in one section of the pattern onto tracing paper, then turn the tracing paper over and trace the design. Repeat to fill the star shape.

DOODLING THE DESIGN

Take the finished origami star and, using tracing paper (or baking parchment), lightly pencil in the outline of the snowflake design. Go over the pencil lines with 0.1mm black fineliner pen, then erase the pencil work.

Use felt-tip pens to block in the background colour.

Use black fineliner pen to draw spots...

then add dots and doodles in silver gel pen!

Outline the pattern with a darker shade of the background colour using felt-tip or fineliner pen.

FESTIVE STARS

Experiment by designing Zen Doodle patterns that combine different elements of the festive season.

I used colours that I associate with winter - white for snow, red and green for holly, and gold for richness and warmth.

Tree decorations.

Snowflakes.

Christmas trees.

Golden stars.

FESTIVE DECORATIONS

SNOW WHITE...

To make a white origami star, start with the paper coloured side up and fold steps 1-15 on pages 68-69. Combine the parts of your roughs that you feel work the best. Pencil in the design using a ruler to draw the geometrical shapes. Then go over the pencil lines with a black 0.1mm fineliner pen.

Leave a white border around the main shapes. Use felt-tip and fineliner pens to block in the colour.

Use a gold gel pen to Zen Doodle the small stars and to embellish the central star. Add detail to the background using a black fineliner pen. For a 3D effect, add shading around the base of the central star using black ballpoint pen.

TREASURED GIFT...

Each star can be a treasured gift for someone special. Or use them for decoration by attaching thin ribbons to the back of your stars using double-sided tape. Hang them on the Christmas tree or in your windows.

ORIGAMI CRANE

According to Japanese legend, anyone who folds one thousand paper cranes will have their heart's desires fulfilled...

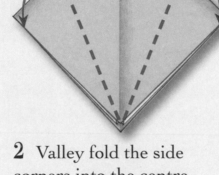

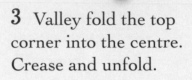

1 With the grey of the paper facing upwards, fold the square base (see page 7).

2 Valley fold the side corners into the centre. Crease and unfold.

3 Valley fold the top corner into the centre. Crease and unfold.

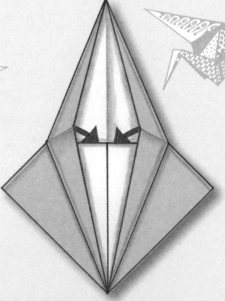

4 Lift the top layer of the bottom point...

5 keep lifting.

6 As the corner rises up, the sides move towards the centre.

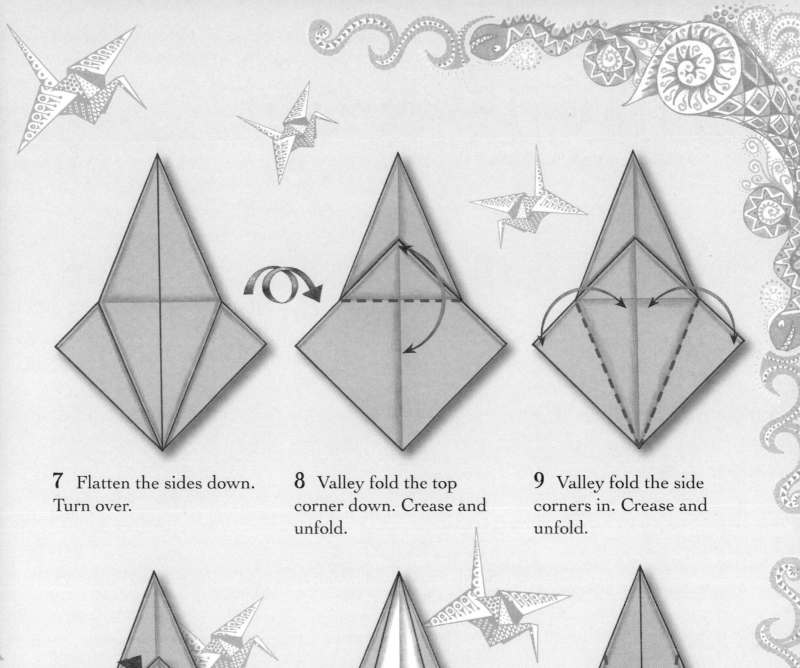

7 Flatten the sides down. Turn over.

8 Valley fold the top corner down. Crease and unfold.

9 Valley fold the side corners in. Crease and unfold.

10 Start to lift up the bottom corner (top layer only).

11 As the corner rises, bring each side in towards the centre. Flatten.

12 Valley fold the top layer of both sides into the centre.

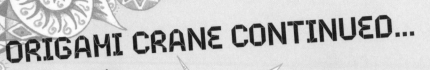

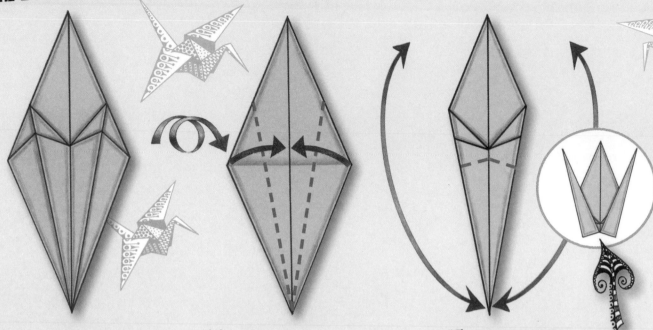

13 Crease, then turn over.

14 Valley fold both sides into the centre and crease.

15 Valley fold both points up at an angle (as shown). Crease and unfold.

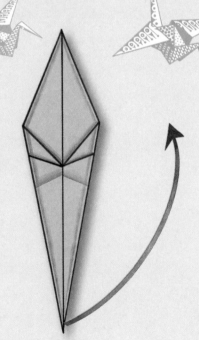

16 Ease one point out sideways.

17 Allow the side to open and use three mountain folds to tuck the point inside.

18 Repeat on the other side of the model.

19 Valley fold the tip. Crease and unfold

To fold the beak:

20 (a) Open up the end. Push down the tip.

20 (b) Pinch the top corners together.

21 Valley fold the wing down. Crease and unfold. Turn over.

22 Valley fold the other wing down. Crease and unfold.

23 Fold both wings down at 90°.

24 Gently pull out the wings.

Finished!

FLIGHTS OF FANCY...

WING STRUCTURE...

Use some scrap paper to fold a paper crane. Try creating Zen Doodles based on feather patterns. I used the shapes formed by a crane's different wing feathers to create the structure for my design.

3D sketch

3D sketch

Black marker pen is ideal for blocking in the long, primary feathers.

PENCILLING IN

Take your original paper crane, fold up the wings and lay it flat. Lightly pencil in the main shapes of your design. Turn the model over and repeat with the other side. Fold down the wings then draw the shape of the patterns on the top side of the wings.

White on Black

Carefully unfold the crane and lay it flat. Now relax and doodle! Use white gel pen and black fineliner pen to block in areas. Add patterns using silver and white gel pens.

Head

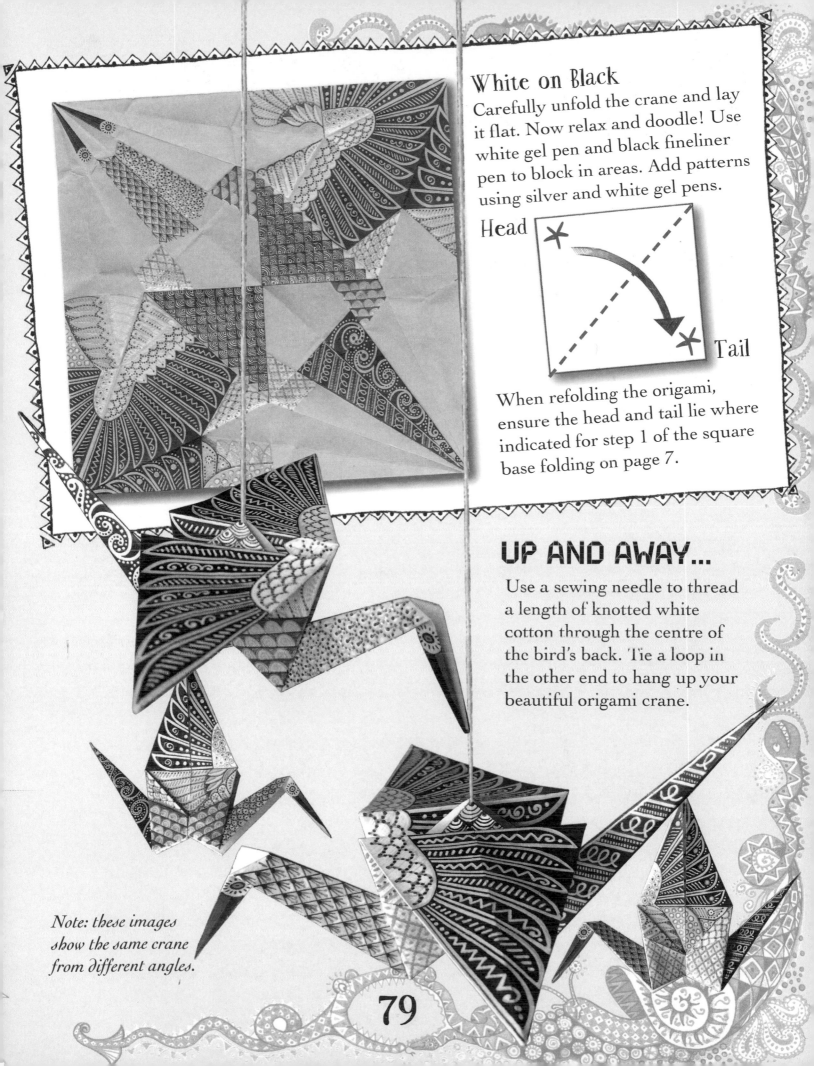

Tail

When refolding the origami, ensure the head and tail lie where indicated for step 1 of the square base folding on page 7.

UP AND AWAY...

Use a sewing needle to thread a length of knotted white cotton through the centre of the bird's back. Tie a loop in the other end to hang up your beautiful origami crane.

Note: these images show the same crane from different angles.

GLOSSARY

Blocking in where areas of flat colour are put down after completion of a sketch or drawing

Colour temperature the coolness or warmth of a colour (blue-green is coldest and red-orange is warmest)

Deconstruct to break down a pattern into simple components

Design a graphic representation usually a drawing or sketch

Hatching a shading technique using a series of parallel lines

Light source the direction from which light shines

Limited palette a restricted number of colours used in artwork

Motif a strong and possibly recurring shape or image in a design

Optical illusion an image that tricks the brain into seeing something different from what is really there

Shading the lines an artist uses to represent gradations of tone

Tonal contrast the difference between the light and dark areas

INDEX